First Workshop on Multimodal Machine Learning in Low-resource Languages (MMLow 2022)

AA004818

New Delhi, India
15 December 2022

ISBN: 978-1-7138-9114-7

Printed from e-media with permission by:

Curran Associates, Inc.
57 Morehouse Lane
Red Hook, NY 12571

Some format issues inherent in the e-media version may also appear in this print version.

Copyright© (2022) by the Association for Computational Linguistics
All rights reserved.

Printed with permission by Curran Associates, Inc. (2024)

For permission requests, please contact the Association for Computational Linguistics at the address below.

Association for Computational Linguistics
209 N. Eighth Street
Stroudsburg, Pennsylvania 18360

Phone: 1-570-476-8006
Fax: 1-570-476-0860

acl@aclweb.org

Additional copies of this publication are available from:

Curran Associates, Inc.
57 Morehouse Lane
Red Hook, NY 12571 USA
Phone: 845-758-0400
Fax: 845-758-2633
Email: curran@proceedings.com
Web: www.proceedings.com

MMLow 2022

First Workshop on Multimodal Machine Learning in Low-resource Languages

Proceedings of the Workshop

December 15, 2022

Introduction

In recent years, the exploitation of the potential of big data has resulted in significant advancements in a variety of Computer Vision and Natural Language Processing applications. However, the majority of tasks addressed thus far have been primarily visual in nature due to the unbalanced availability of labelled samples across modalities (e.g., there are numerous large labelled datasets for images but few for audio or IMU-based classification), resulting in a large performance gap when algorithms are trained separately. With its origins in audio-visual speech recognition and, more recently, in language and vision projects such as image and video captioning, multimodal machine learning is a thriving multidisciplinary research field that addresses several of artificial intelligence's (AI) original goals by integrating and modelling multiple communicative modalities, including linguistic, acoustic, and visual messages. Due to the variability of the data and the frequently observed dependency between modalities, this study subject presents some particular problems for machine learning researchers. Because the majority of this hateful content is in regional languages, they easily slip past online surveillance algorithms that are designed to target articles written in resource-rich languages like English. As a result, low-resource regional languages in Asia, Africa, Europe, and South America face a shortage of tools, benchmark datasets, and machine learning approaches.

This workshop aims to bring together members of the machine learning and multimodal data fusion fields in regional languages. We anticipate contributions that hate speech and emotional analysis in multimodality include video, audio, text, drawings, and synthetic material in regional language. This workshop's objective is to advance scientific study in the broad field of multimodal interaction, techniques, and systems, emphasising important trends and difficulties in regional languages, with a goal of developing a roadmap for future research and commercial success.

We invite submissions on topics that include, but are not limited to, the following: (a) Multimodal Sentiment Analysis in regional languages (b) Hate content video detection in regional languages (c) Trolling and Offensive post detection in Memes (d) Multimodal data fusion and data representation for hate speech detection in regional language (e) Multimodal hate speech benchmark datasets and evaluations in regional languages (f) Multimodal fake news in regional languages (g) Data collection and annotation methodologies for safer social media in low-resourced languages (h) Content moderation strategies in regional languages (i) Cybersecurity and social media in regional languages

We received 16 papers after a careful review process; two papers were selected for the proceedings.

Organizing Committee

Workshop Organizers

Bharathi Raja Chakravarthi, University of Galway, Ireland
Abirami Murugappan, Anna University, Chennai, India
Dhivya Chinnappa, Thomson Reuters, USA
Adeep Hande, Indiana University Bloomington, IN, USA
Prasanna Kumar Kumaresan, Indian Institute of Information Technology and Management- Kerala, India
Rahul Ponnusamy, Techvantage Analytics, India

Invited Speakers

Desmond Elliot, University of Copenhagen, Denmark
Shyamala Doraisamy, Universiti Putra Malaysia, Malaysia

Program Committee

Program Committee

Muzhaffar Hazman, University of Galway, Ireland
Premjith B, Amrita Vishwa Vidyapeetham, India
Sumana Biswas, University of Galway, Ireland
Bharathi B, SSN College of Engineering, India
Manoj Balaji J, Deloitte, India
Premjith B, Amrita Vishwa Vidyapeetham, India
Thenmozhi Durairaj, SSN College of Engineering, India
Anand Kumar M, National Institute of Technology Karnataka, India
Subalalitha C N, SRM Institute of Science and Technology, India
Rajalakshmi Ratnavel, Vellore Institute of Technology, Chennai, India
Antonette Shibani Xavier, University of Technology Sydney, Australia

Table of Contents

Multimodal Code-Mixed Tamil Troll Meme Classification using Feature Fusion

R.Ramesh Kannan, Ratnavel Rajalakshmi ∗
School of Computer Science and Engineering, Vellore Institute of Technology, Chennai, India
ramesh.kannan2018@vitstudent.ac.in, rajalakshmi.r@vit.ac.in

Abstract

Memes became an important way of expressing relevant idea through social media platforms and forums. At the same time, these memes are trolled by a person who tries to get identified from the other internet users like social media users, chat rooms and blogs. The memes contain both textual and visual information. Based on the content of memes, they are trolled in online community. There is no restriction for language usage in online media. The present work focuses on whether memes are trolled or not trolled. The proposed multi modal approach achieved considerably better weighted average F1 score of 0.5437 compared to Unimodal approaches. The other performance metrics like precision, recall, accuracy and macro average have also been studied to observe the proposed system.

1 Introduction

Social Media is a technology where people share information, idea and their opinions to the virtual group of people. These contents uses internet to reach the people via electronic medium, which includes photos, videos, and textual information (Chakravarthi and Muralidaran, 2021; Chakravarthi et al., 2022). These electronic social media contents are accessed through computers, mobiles, tablets via the web based applications (Hande et al., 2022; Shanmugavadivel et al., 2022; Subramanian et al., 2022). Government keep an eye on the conventional media contents, because the information shared in conventional media are monitored for trolled contents (Chakravarthi, 2020, 2022b,a). But in case of social media there is no strict laws or methodologies to monitor the internet contents.

One of the most important way of sharing our thought is either via text messages or via images. There are so many contributions for social media contents like text, emojis, info graphics, charts and photographs. In this, photographs and texts plays a key role. Meme is an element of behaviour imitation passed from an individual to another. Meme was first coined by British evolutionary biologist Richard Dawkins in 1976 (ric). It is an idea to mutate, replicate or imitate others behaviours to pass an information. It is an art of writing human creativity.

Memes with text and images could be detected for trolled or not trolled. Visual question answering, image captioning (Biswas et al., 2020) and identifying the images are categorised as classification problem that depends both on the individual inputs. This type of classification task is portrayed in Troll meme classification in Tamil (Beltrán et al., 2021) (Suryawanshi et al., 2020). This task focuses on memes as trolled or not trolled. The idea of trolled is determined by the text and image interaction as shown in Figure 1-2.

Authors handled the multi modal input data for different applications such as Hateful Meme detection (Evtimov et al., 2020) and adversarial Meme detection (Lippe et al., 2020) . Particularly the Figure 1 shows that the event happened in recent times with popular occurrences/offensive texts are get trolled. But in case of 2 is not an recent time activity happened does not contain any harm or offensive messages that are not get trolled.

Meme is a good imitation of a real world problem. Here the task on Troll meme classification in Tamil is a task of classifying the memes into hate and non hate images. Troll is nothing but a offensive message or disruptive message in the social media. The language mentioned in the task is Tamil. For the text memes, corresponding image memes also given. By using the texts and the images, the proposed system need to classify whether the meme is trolled or not. The evaluation metric from the data set is taken as weighted F1 score.

In this research, we have defined the research

Proceedings of the Workshop on Multimodal Machine Learning in Low-resource Languages, pages 1 - 8
December 15, 2022 ©2022 Association for Computational Linguistics

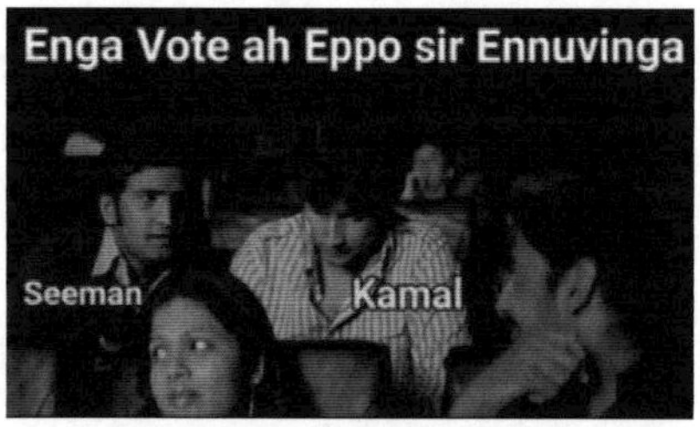

Figure 1: Example image for Troll meme

Figure 2: Example image for Non Troll meme

Figure 1 is trolled and Figure 2 is not trolled image. Figure 1-Enga vote ah eppa sir enuvinga which is in tanglish is transliterated as *"when will you count our vote sir"*, Figure 2- ungala maari oru friend kadaikka naan romba koduthu vechirukkanu in tanglish is transliterated as *"it would be great to have a friend like you..."*

questions and the same have been addressed in the next upcoming sections. Research Question 1: To study the performance of the pretrained word embedding like GloVe for transliterated content. Research Question 2: Analyse the performance of the GloVe embedding with other language based pretrained models Research Question 3: To study the performance of the system with the Deep learning architectures with GloVe embeddings. To solve the research questions, extensive literature study have been conducted and reported.

This section describes about the introduction and Section 2 and 3 talks about the related works and methodologies used in the classification task. Section 4 describes the results and discussion and last section deals with Conclusion of the paper.

2 Related Works

Multimodal representation have recently gained good attention due to the uni modals (Suryawanshi et al., 2020) poor performance on the applications such as image captioning (Biswas et al., 2020), visual reasoning (Ye, 2021) , memes classification and Visual question answering (Cadène et al., 2019). Multimodal task involves visual and language understanding between the two Unimodalities. Maximum works carried on Multimodal systems have either one is Late fusion (LF) (Snoek et al., 2005) or Early fusion (EF) (Sai et al., 2022). The other fusion techniques are Hybrid multimodal fusion, Model-level fusion, Rule-based fusion, Classification-based fusion, Estimation-based fusion are reported in the literature survey (Poria et al., 2017). Late fusion process involves two unimodal system independently till before the last layer and fuse the their decisions for further processing. Early fusion approach uses two modalities with complex approaches within the model architectures. Early fusion of the features provide better representation for further processing in accomplishing the task. Some of the steps are followed in NLP type of task are pre-processing , feature engineering, and dimensionality reduction. Preprocessing involves stop word removal, tokenization, spelling correction, noise removal, remove numbers, stemming and lemmeatization. For English memes (Suryawanshi et al., 2020) these types of pre processings are applicable, but in case of non English memes some other type of pre processing be used to clean the input data. Applied stop word removal and special characters removed on transliterated dataset content. Feature engineering is used to extract useful features from the input data. Some of the feature engineering word embedding approaches are GloVe, Word2Vec, Ngram and Term frequency and Inverse Document frequency. Dimensionality reduction technique used to reduce the dimensionality of the large data sets into a smaller data set which may contain the most important features from large data set. For social media comments (Kannan et al., 2021; Soubraylu and Rajalakshmi, 2021a; Rajalakshmi et al., 2021), different transformer based approaches and attention based approach are proposed. Many researchers have implemented classifiers such as KNN, Naive Bayes,SVM and Ensemble classifiers (Rajalakshmi et al., 2022c; Rajalakshmi and Reddy, 2019).

Recently Deep Learning (DL) methods such as RNN, CNN and transformer models (Devlin et al., 2018; Liu et al., 2019; Lan et al., 2020; Gurari et al., 2020), BiLSTM-CRF(Rajalakshmi et al., 2022b) and hybrid convolutional bidirectional recurrent neural network for sentiment analysis(Soubraylu and Rajalakshmi, 2021b) attains better results compared to Machine learning models due to ability to model complex representations inside the data.

Image classification on meme classification starts with the pre processing steps like resize the image, noise removal, RGB2Gray scale conversion and segmentation process. After pre processing feature extraction involves color extraction, texture extraction, shape and deep feature extraction. For short text classification task (Rajalakshmi et al., 2020a), proposed CNN with Bi-GRU on Open Directory Project (ODP) dataset and obtained 82.04% accuracy.

(Ganganwar and Rajalakshmi, 2022; Rajalakshmi et al., 2021, 2023) studied the performance of transformers on the code-mixed social media contents. (Ganganwar and Rajalakshmi, 2022) proposed translation based offensive content identification on Tamil text using pretrained word embedding. MuRIL pretrained embeddings were used by the translated content for classification. In (Rajalakshmi and Agrawal, 2017), authors proposed relevance based metric for code-mixed language by using statistics based approach. (Rajalakshmi et al., 2021) proposed transformer based approach for identification of offensive content on social media Tamil comments. In (Soubraylu and Rajalakshmi, 2022), the authors proposed transfer learning approach for movie review by using Bidirectional Gate Recurrent Unit(BGRU). The features from BERT embeddings are used as features for transfer learning approach. (Rajalakshmi et al., 2023) proposed MuRIL based approach for YouTube comments for offensive content identification. (Ravikiran et al., 2022) created dataset for offensive span identification for Code-Mixed social media Tamil contents. (Rajalakshmi, 2014, 2015; Rajalakshmi and Aravindan, 2018; Rajalakshmi and Xaviar, 2017; Rajalakshmi et al., 2020b) Traditional machine learning algorithms and text embedding methods (Rajalakshmi et al., 2018) have been proposed on short text classifications. Transformer based approach (Rajalakshmi et al., 2022a) and XGBoost (Sharen and Rajalakshmi, 2022) based approaches were used on depression detection using signs. Aspect-based approach (Ganganwar and Rajalakshmi, 2019) is studied on sentiment analysis.

Most of the image classifier models uses Convolutional Neural Network (CNN) architecture for feature extraction, which automatically extracts the features from the data inputs. MobileNetV2 (Sandler et al., 2018) pre-trained model uses these automatic feature extraction of deep learning model with depth wise convolution and point wise convolution for reducing the parameters. In our Multimodal classifier approach, the proposed system used CNN with Bidirectional Long Short Term Memory (Bi-LSTM) as text classifier and MobileNetV2 as image classifier for troll meme classification with multimodal approach. A detailed experimental study has been conducted to explore the role of CNN, Bi-LSTM and combination of both. CNN works well for short text analysis in English (Rajalakshmi et al., 2020a). To explore the role of CNN for our application we adapted the same to our approach. MobileNetV2 is very effective feature extractor for image classification problems better than VGG and ResNet. So we have adopted both to our proposed architecture.

3 Methodology

3.1 Data Set

The data set provided for the Troll Meme classification (Suryawanshi and Chakravarthi, 2021) with 2300 as training data with text and image inputs and 667 as test set inputs. 2100 inputs are taken for training and 200 for validation process. Here the data set is splitted into around 80% for training and 20% for testing. For validation set 9% of the data taken from training set. Data set contains trolled/not trolled texts and images of trolled/not trolled images and their corresponding labels. Figure 1 is trolled image with text as **"Enga vote ah eppa sir enuvinga"** which is in tanglish is transliterated as **"when will you count our vote sir"** and Figure 2 is not trolled image with text as **"ungala maari oru friend kadaikka naan romba koduthu vechirukkanu"** in tanglish is transliterated as **"it would be great to have a friend like you..."**

Table 1: Data Set Description

Data Set	Troll	Not Troll	Total
Training	1182	918	2100
Validation	100	100	200
Testing	395	272	667

3.2 Architecture

Deep learning architectures CNN and Bi-LSTM are used for text classification, which uses CNN for feature extraction and Bi-LSTM in both the directions to capture the sequence of the text representations. LSTM (Long Short Term Memory) captures the next sequence in unidirectional way.

but in case of Bi-LSTM, it is used to find the next sequence of words in both the directions. CNN used to capture the important features from the text data and the same is passed to Bi-LSTM to maintain the sequence of the statement. Meme's texts contains Tamil words transliterated in English. Syntactic and semantic meaning of Tamil words in native languages are completely different than English, but in case for Meme's, the messages are represented in Tamil, English and Tanglish (Tamil+English) representations are transliterated and represented in English . The dataset with image may contain Tamil texts, but the data set released with transliterated format of the Meme's texts.

GloVe (Global Vectors for word representation) vector with 50 dimension is used for obtaining vector representations of input sequences. We have tried other GloVe embedding dimensions such as 50, 100, 200. In addition to GloVe embedding, we have tried with IndicBERT and mBERT approaches and achieved 0.5379 and 0.5219 respectively. 50 dimension shown better performance on the Meme's text architecture. This is used to get the global word occurrence statistics from the corpus. Maximum length of the sequence is set as 150. The architecture followed with Input layer, embedding layer, CNN, Bi-LSTM. The sequence information from Bi-LSTM is given as input to Global Average pooling layer and Max pooling layer separately and concatenated towards dense layer followed by dropout and dense layer. Number of units in the Bi-LSTM is 200 units, CNN with kernel size as 3, filter size 30 are selected with hyper parameter tuning. Sigmoid activation function is used since it is a binary classification.

Table 2: Meme Classification based on Text

Class	Precision	Recall	F1
Not Troll	0.4324	0.3529	0.3887
Troll	0.6045	0.6810	0.6405
M.Avg	0.5185	0.5170	0.5146
W.Avg	0.5343	0.5472	0.5378

For Image classification, pretrained image classification model MobileNetV2 (Sandler et al., 2018) is used, which uses expanded representations in light weight depth wise manner. It uses convolution layers to filter out the features from the intermediate layers of the model. It removes non linearities to represent the features of the input data. The extracted features from the meme images and the extracted features with text features are fused for further processing. Images in the meme classification are with input size of 150. Figure 1 is a trolled image contains trolled messages in the text form. But in case of not trolled image (Figure 2) are only expressions, that may or may not contain the trolled message. So troll meme classification in Tamil is not like a regular image classification problem. With the help of text only input does not enough to develop the system. With the help of images and text can develop better system for troll meme classification. Early fusion is applied on multi modal data inputs build a multi modal classifier. concatenated features are given to dense layer for final classification.

4 Results and Discussion

Table 2, shows the classification of the text input with the Deep learning approach of CNN with Bi-LSTM model which achieved a weighted F1 score of 0.5378 for text input data. The model trained for 25 epochs and obtained a training accuracy of 0.8905 and loss of 0.3054. The validation set obtained a accuracy of 0.6714 and loss of 0.7057 on Meme's texts with a batch size of 128 and sigmoid as activation function. The recall score for Troll Meme text is shown with 0.6810 score, because the model has identified around 68% of the Troll text correctly. The precision score shown as 0.6045 for the Troll text. The macro average score shows an overall performance of the system with each metrics.

Table 3: Meme Classification based on Image

Class	Precision	Recall	F1
Not Troll	0.4202	0.4743	0.4456
Troll	0.6028	0.5494	0.5748
M.Avg	0.5115	0.5118	0.5102
W.Avg	0.5283	0.5187	0.5221

Image classification on troll meme achieved a weighted average F1 score of 0.5221 and precision as 0.5283 and recall as 0.518 on troll image classification for the MobileNetV2 architecture. This image classification model, which uses pre-trained model of MobileNetV2 for feature extraction in depth wise and point wise convolutions. From Table 3, trolled images are classified better than not trolled images. because of the meme images may not contain same set of pattern on images for feature extraction. Obtained a training accuracy of 0.9810 and validation accuracy of 0.9652. The same model obtained a loss of 0.0612, 0.1760 on training set and validation set respectively. The table shown overall Troll classified images with 60% from the test set.

Table 4: Meme Classification based on Multimodal

Class	Precision	Recall	F1
Not Troll	0.4402	0.3787	0.4071
Troll	0.6097	0.6684	0.6377
M.Avg	0.5249	0.5235	0.5224
W.Avg	0.5406	0.5502	0.5437

Table 5: Comparison Result on Multimodal

Multimodal	Result
BiGRU+CNN	0.4 (Huang and Bai, 2021)
Bert+ViT	0.47 (Hegde et al., 2021)
Bi-LSTM+CNN	0.525 (Hossain et al., 2021)
Our Approach	**0.5437**

Early Fusion on Multimodal classification achieved 0.5437 weighted average F1 score on troll memes, which is a 1% increase in the performance of Unimodal classifications. Table 4, shows the results of Multimodal meme classification results. We have conducted 4 fold and 5 fold cross validation for text contents and image contents. The CNN-Bi-LSTM approach obtained overall cross validation of 71.24% and 73.81% on 4 fold and 5 fold training sets. The same has been conducted to test and obtained 54.46% and 54.27% for 4 fold and 5 fold respectively. The same cross validation has been conducted on MobileNetV2 to verify the system performance. 4 fold cross validation obtained 55.74% and 59.22% on train set and test respectively. 5 fold cross validation on train set obtained 55.87% and 59.22% on test set respectively. From this the obtained results using the full training set is consistent with the cross validation score performance.

From Table 5, the comparison of our approach with other approaches on the same data set has been discussed. (Huang and Bai, 2021) proposed fusion approach with Bidirectional GRU (BGRU) for Text classification and Convolutional Neural Network (CNN) for image classification and obtained 0.4 of F1 score. (Hegde et al., 2021) used the same data set and obtained 0.47 using Bidirectional Encoder Representations from Transformers (BERT) for Text classification and Vision Transformer (ViT) for Image classification with Early fusion. (Hossain et al., 2021) used Bi-LSTM for meme Text classification and CNN for Image classification and obtained 0.525 F1 score. From the above mentioned results our approach on Multimodal Meme classification obtained a F1 Score of 0.5437 using CNN-Bi-LSTM for Text classification and MobileNetV2 for image classification. Sequence features are extracted using Bi-LSTM and other features are extracted using CNN in trolled messages. pre-trained MobileNetV2 architecture used to extract the features from Trolled image data sets. Both features are concatenated to form a new feature vector space and classified as multimodal analysis. By this, Multimodal classifiers results are better than Unimodal classifiers on text and image inputs.

From our results, the recall value for Troll text and images shown higher results compared to precision on all the unimodal approaches. Because all the images on the data set contains shown very few false negatives. It means that troll categories are classified almost correctly. We need to concentrate more on Non troll contents of both text and images to improve the performance of the system. On comparing the results of the recall on unimodal and Multimodal approach, the image classifier classified more Troll images in terms of True category. For Non troll category all the modals have higher precision score than recall score.

Statistical significance test, Fried man test is conducted for our proposed architecture with other two unimodal approaches. Null Hypothesis h0 and different alternate hypothesis H1 is defined and computed the score. For 10 instances and level of significance as 0.01 is observed on Fried table and obtained Fr as 9.60. We have populated the table with respective rankings and calculated the score as 72.9. This is greater than 9.60 of table value. So we can accept the alternate hypothesis. This assessment tool is used the test the performance of the proposed system with other systems.

5 Conclusion

Combination of sequence based model and pre-trained image model showed better performance. CNN-Bi-LSTM classifier on text input and MobileNetV2 on image input combination obtained some better performance on multimodal approach.

The GloVe embedding performance on troll classification shown better performance with Deep Learning architectures. In order to obtain better result, the multimodal approach shown some better performance than the unimodal approaches. The performance metrics weighted F1 score is chosen to balance the results on the both class labels. Weighted average on meme classification gives important to both the classes. By using Multimodal classification approach on memes attained a result of 0.5437 weighted F1 score. The performance of the Multimodal classifier can be improved with more number of input data and feature extraction on images. The dataset is created on low-resource language Tamil and the cultural adaptation details can be considered for future scope.

References

https://www.themarginalian.org/2013/10/02/richard-dawkins-meme-appetite-for-wonder/.

L. Viviana Beltrán Beltrán, Juan C. Caicedo, Nicholas Journet, Mickaël Coustaty, François Lecellier, and Antoine Doucet. 2021. Deep multimodal learning for cross-modal retrieval: One model for all tasks. *Pattern Recognition Letters*, 146:38–45.

Rajarshi Biswas, Michael Barz, and Daniel Sonntag. 2020. Towards explanatory interactive image captioning using top-down and bottom-up features, beam search and re-ranking. *KI - Künstliche Intelligenz*, 34:1–14.

Rémi Cadène, Hédi Ben-Younes, Matthieu Cord, and Nicolas Thome. 2019. MUREL: multimodal relational reasoning for visual question answering. *CoRR*, abs/1902.09487.

Bharathi Raja Chakravarthi. 2020. HopeEDI: A multilingual hope speech detection dataset for equality, diversity, and inclusion. In *Proceedings of the Third Workshop on Computational Modeling of People's Opinions, Personality, and Emotion's in Social Media*, pages 41–53, Barcelona, Spain (Online). Association for Computational Linguistics.

Bharathi Raja Chakravarthi. 2022a. Hope speech detection in youtube comments. *Social Network Analysis and Mining*, 12(1):1–19.

Bharathi Raja Chakravarthi. 2022b. Multilingual hope speech detection in English and Dravidian languages. *International Journal of Data Science and Analytics*, 14(4):389–406.

Bharathi Raja Chakravarthi, Adeep Hande, Rahul Ponnusamy, Prasanna Kumar Kumaresan, and Ruba Priyadharshini. 2022. How can we detect homophobia and transphobia? experiments in a multilingual code-mixed setting for social media governance. *International Journal of Information Management Data Insights*, 2(2):100119.

Bharathi Raja Chakravarthi and Vigneshwaran Muralidaran. 2021. Findings of the shared task on hope speech detection for equality, diversity, and inclusion. In *Proceedings of the First Workshop on Language Technology for Equality, Diversity and Inclusion*, pages 61–72, Kyiv. Association for Computational Linguistics.

Jacob Devlin, Ming-Wei Chang, Kenton Lee, and Kristina Toutanova. 2018. BERT: pre-training of deep bidirectional transformers for language understanding. *CoRR*, abs/1810.04805.

Ivan Evtimov, Russ Howes, Brian Dolhansky, Hamed Firooz, and Cristian Canton-Ferrer. 2020. Adversarial evaluation of multimodal models under realistic gray box assumption. *CoRR*, abs/2011.12902.

Vaishali Ganganwar and R Rajalakshmi. 2019. Implicit aspect extraction for sentiment analysis: a survey of recent approaches. *Procedia Computer Science*, 165:485–491.

Vaishali Ganganwar and Ratnavel Rajalakshmi. 2022. Mtdot: A multilingual translation-based data augmentation technique for offensive content identification in tamil text data. *Electronics*, 11(21).

Danna Gurari, Yinan Zhao, Meng Zhang, and Nilavra Bhattacharya. 2020. Captioning images taken by people who are blind. In *Computer Vision – ECCV 2020*, pages 417–434, Cham. Springer International Publishing.

Adeep Hande, Siddhanth U Hegde, and Bharathi Raja Chakravarthi. 2022. Multi-task learning in under-resourced dravidian languages. *Journal of Data, Information and Management*, 4(2):137–165.

Siddhanth U. Hegde, Adeep Hande, Ruba Priyadarshini, Sajeetha Thavareesan, and Bharathi Raja Chakravarthi. 2021. UVCE-IIITT@DravidianLangTech-EACL2021: Tamil Troll Meme Classification: You need to Pay more Attention. *Proceedings of the 1st Workshop on Speech and Language Technologies for Dravidian Languages, DravidianLangTech 2021 at 16th Conference of the European Chapter of the Association for Computational Linguistics, EACL 2021*, pages 180–186.

Eftekhar Hossain, Omar Sharif, and Mohammed Moshiul Hoque. 2021. NLP-CUET@DravidianLangTech-EACL2021: Investigating visual and textual features to identify trolls from multimodal social media memes. In *Proceedings of the First Workshop on Speech and Language Technologies for Dravidian Languages*, pages 300–306, Kyiv. Association for Computational Linguistics.

Bo Huang and Yang Bai. 2021. HUB@DravidianLangTech-EACL2021: Meme classification for Tamil text-image fusion. In *Proceedings of the First Workshop on Speech and Language Technologies for Dravidian Languages*, pages 210–215, Kyiv. Association for Computational Linguistics.

R Ramesh Kannan, Ratnavel Rajalakshmi, and Lokesh Kumar. 2021. Indicbert based approach for sentiment analysis on code-mixed tamil tweets. 3159:8.

Zhenzhong Lan, Mingda Chen, Sebastian Goodman, Kevin Gimpel, Piyush Sharma, and Radu Soricut. 2020. Albert: A lite bert for self-supervised learning of language representations. In *International Conference on Learning Representations*.

Phillip Lippe, Nithin Holla, Shantanu Chandra, Santhosh Rajamanickam, Georgios Antoniou, Ekaterina Shutova, and Helen Yannakoudakis. 2020. A multimodal framework for the detection of hateful memes. *CoRR*, abs/2012.12871.

Yinhan Liu, Myle Ott, Naman Goyal, Jingfei Du, Mandar Joshi, Danqi Chen, Omer Levy, Mike Lewis, Luke Zettlemoyer, and Veselin Stoyanov. 2019. Roberta: A robustly optimized BERT pretraining approach. *CoRR*, abs/1907.11692.

Soujanya Poria, Erik Cambria, Rajiv Bajpai, and Amir Hussain. 2017. A review of affective computing: From unimodal analysis to multimodal fusion. *Information Fusion*, 37:98–125.

R. Rajalakshmi and B. Yashwant Reddy. 2019. DLRG@hasoc 2019: An enhanced ensemble classifier for hate and offensive content identification. In *Working Notes of FIRE 2019 - Forum for Information Retrieval Evaluation, Kolkata, India, December 12-15, 2019*, volume 2517 of *CEUR Workshop Proceedings*, pages 370–379. CEUR-WS.org.

R. Rajalakshmi, Hans Tiwari, Jay Patel, Ankit Kumar, and R Karthik. 2020a. Design of kids-specific url classifier using recurrent convolutional neural network. *Proceedia Computer Science*, 167:2124–2131. International Conference on Computational Intelligence and Data Science.

R Rajalakshmi, Hans Tiwari, Jay Patel, Ankit Kumar, and R Karthik. 2020b. Design of kids-specific URL classifier using Recurrent Convolutional Neural Network. *Procedia Computer Science*, 167:2124–2131.

R Rajalakshmi and Sanju Xaviar. 2017. Experimental study of feature weighting techniques for URL based webpage classification. *Procedia computer science*, 115:218–225.

Ratnavel Rajalakshmi. 2014. Supervised term weighting methods for URL classification. *J. Comput. Sci.*, 10(10):1969–1976.

Ratnavel Rajalakshmi. 2015. Identifying health domain URLs using SVM. In *Proceedings of the Third International Symposium on Women in Computing and Informatics*, pages 203–208.

Ratnavel Rajalakshmi and Rohan Agrawal. 2017. Borrowing likeliness ranking based on relevance factor. In *Proceedings of the Fourth ACM IKDD Conferences on Data Sciences*, pages 1–2.

Ratnavel Rajalakshmi and Chandrabose Aravindan. 2018. An effective and discriminative feature learning for URL based web page classification. In *2018 IEEE International Conference on Systems, Man, and Cybernetics (SMC)*, pages 1374–1379. IEEE.

Ratnavel Rajalakshmi, Ankita Duraphe, and Antonette Shibani. 2022a. DLRG@ DravidianLangTech-ACL2022: Abusive comment detection in tamil using multilingual transformer models. In *Proceedings of the Second Workshop on Speech and Language Technologies for Dravidian Languages*, pages 207–213.

Ratnavel Rajalakshmi, Mohit More, Bhamatipati Shrikriti, Gitansh Saharan, Hanchate Samyuktha, and Sayantan Nandy. 2022b. DLRG@ tamilnlp-acl2022: Offensive span identification in Tamil using BiLSTM-CRF approach. In *Proceedings of the Second Workshop on Speech and Language Technologies for Dravidian Languages*, pages 248–253.

Ratnavel Rajalakshmi, S Ramraj, and R Ramesh Kannan. 2018. Transfer learning approach for identification of malicious domain names. In *International Symposium on Security in Computing and Communication*, pages 656–666. Springer.

Ratnavel Rajalakshmi, Preethi Reddy, Shreya Khare, and Vaishali Ganganwar. 2022c. Sentimental analysis of code-mixed Hindi language. In *Congress on Intelligent Systems*, pages 739–751. Springer.

Ratnavel Rajalakshmi, Yashwant Reddy, and Lokesh Kumar. 2021. DLRG@DravidianLangTech-EACL2021: Transformer based approach for offensive language identification on code-mixed Tamil. In *Proceedings of the First Workshop on Speech and Language Technologies for Dravidian Languages*, pages 357–362, Kyiv. Association for Computational Linguistics.

Ratnavel Rajalakshmi, Srivarshan Selvaraj, Faerie Mattins R., Pavitra Vasudevan, and Anand Kumar M. 2023. Hottest: Hate and offensive content identification in tamil using transformers and enhanced stemming. *Computer Speech Language*, 78:101464.

Manikandan Ravikiran, Bharathi Raja Chakravarthi, Anand Kumar Madasamy, Sangeetha S, Ratnavel Rajalakshmi, Sajeetha Thavareesan, Rahul Ponnusamy, and Shankar Mahadevan. 2022. Findings of the shared task on offensive span identification fromCode-mixed Tamil-English comments. In *Proceedings of the Second Workshop on Speech and Language Technologies for Dravidian Languages*, pages

261–270, Dublin, Ireland. Association for Computational Linguistics.

Siva Sai, Naman Srivastava, and Yashvardhan Sharma. 2022. Explorative application of fusion techniques for multimodal hate speech detection. *SN Computer Science*, 3.

Mark Sandler, Andrew G. Howard, Menglong Zhu, Andrey Zhmoginov, and Liang-Chieh Chen. 2018. Mobilenetv2: Inverted residuals and linear bottlenecks. *2018 IEEE/CVF Conference on Computer Vision and Pattern Recognition*, pages 4510–4520.

Kogilavani Shanmugavadivel, Sai Haritha Sampath, Pramod Nandhakumar, Prasath Mahalingam, Malliga Subramanian, Prasanna Kumar Kumaresan, and Ruba Priyadharshini. 2022. An analysis of machine learning models for sentiment analysis of tamil code-mixed data. *Computer Speech & Language*, page 101407.

Herbert Sharen and Ratnavel Rajalakshmi. 2022. DLRG@ LT-EDI-ACL2022: Detecting signs of depression from social media using XGBoost method. In *Proceedings of the Second Workshop on Language Technology for Equality, Diversity and Inclusion*, pages 346–349.

C. G. M. Snoek, M. Worring, and A. W. M. Smeulders. 2005. Early versus late fusion in semantic video analysis. In *ACM International Conference on Multimedia*, pages 399—-402.

Sivakumar Soubraylu and Ratnavel Rajalakshmi. 2021a. Analysis of sentiment on movie reviews using word embedding self-attentive lstm. *International Journal of Ambient Computing and Intelligence*, 12:33–52.

Sivakumar Soubraylu and Ratnavel Rajalakshmi. 2021b. Hybrid convolutional bidirectional recurrent neural network based sentiment analysis on movie reviews. *Computational Intelligence*, 37(2):735–757.

Sivakumar Soubraylu and Ratnavel Rajalakshmi. 2022. Context-aware sentiment analysis with attention-enhanced features from bidirectional transformers. *Social Network Analysis and Mining*, 12(1):1–23.

Malliga Subramanian, Rahul Ponnusamy, Sean Benhur, Kogilavani Shanmugavadivel, Adhithiya Ganesan, Deepti Ravi, Gowtham Krishnan Shanmugasundaram, Ruba Priyadharshini, and Bharathi Raja Chakravarthi. 2022. Offensive language detection in tamil YouTube comments by adapters and cross-domain knowledge transfer. *Computer Speech & Language*, 76:101404.

Shardul Suryawanshi and Bharathi Raja Chakravarthi. 2021. Findings of the shared task on Troll Meme Classification in Tamil. In *Proceedings of the First Workshop on Speech and Language Technologies for Dravidian Languages*. Association for Computational Linguistics.

Shardul Suryawanshi, Bharathi Raja Chakravarthi, Mihael Arcan, and Paul Buitelaar. 2020. Multimodal meme dataset (MultiOFF) for identifying offensive content in image and text. In *Proceedings of the Second Workshop on Trolling, Aggression and Cyberbullying*, pages 32–41, Marseille, France. European Language Resources Association (ELRA).

Keren Ye. 2021. Multimodal knowledge integration for object detection and visual reasoning.

Understanding the role of Emojis for emotion detection in Tamil

Ratnavel Rajalakshmi [1,*], Faerie Mattins R[1], Srivarshan Selvaraj[1], Antonette Shibani[2], Anand Kumar M[3], Bharathi Raja Chakravarthi[‡]

[1] School of Computer Science and Engineering, Vellore Institute of Technology, Chennai
[2] University of Technology Sydney, Sydney
[3] National Institute of Technology Karnataka Surathkal.
[‡]School of Computer Science, University of Galway, Ireland
rajalakshmi.r@vit.ac.in, faeriemattins.r2019@vitstudent.ac.in,
srivarshan.2019@vitstudent.ac.in, Antonette.Shibani@uts.edu.au,
manandkumar@nitk.edu.in
bharathiraja.asokachakravarthi@universityofgalway.ie

Abstract

Emotions are commonly discerned by a persons facial expression and body movements. Detecting emotion only through text using Natural language processing (NLP) is a challenging research area for low-resource languages like Tamil. One way to identify emotion is with the help of emojis that are indicative of the emotion expressed by the writer. This paper presents a study on how emojis represent emotion in text and their usage in building machine-learning techniques to detect emotion. Feature extraction techniques like TF-IDF and MuRIL are used with classifiers like Logistic Regression, Random Forest, and XGBoost to detect emotions in Tamil YouTube comments. The most commonly used emojis and the number of times an emoji is repeated in a specific text are analyzed, as well as how they relate to emotion recognition. A combination of TF-IDF and XGBoost achieves the best performance of 0.32 weighted-average F1 score, with the emojis in the text substituted with phrases that depict them.

1 Introduction

The technique of recognizing a person's emotional state of mind by facial expression and demeanor is known as emotion detection (ED) (Chakravarthi and Muralidaran, 2021; Chakravarthi et al., 2022). Detecting a person's emotion in the text is difficult since it seldom provides phrases that explicitly stress the individual's feelings, and emotion is only discovered by interception of concepts through text data. ED is critical in many rapidly evolving fields including e-commerce, social media, comprehensive search, and advertising. Despite past work on ED including speech and facial expressions, text-based ED is limited (Acheampong et al., 2020). Furthermore, ED in Tamil texts is harder than in English due to the scarcity of corpora and NLP tools for low resource languages like Tamil (Thavareesan and Mahesan, 2019, 2020a,b).

People comment on posts/videos on social media sites such as Twitter, YouTube, and Instagram and express their emotions (Chakravarthi, 2020, 2022a,b). Because facial expressions cannot be observed in writing, emojis can be used to infer how the person is feeling (Hande et al., 2022; Shanmugavadivel et al., 2022; Subramanian et al., 2022). Emoji usage is also quite widespread on social media since it allows individuals to express themselves. However, little progress has been made in comprehending the significance of emojis in ED in texts, particularly in low-resource languages like Tamil. Along with the fundamental emotions of fear, anger, joy, sorrow, disgust, and surprise (Cherbonnier and Michinov, 2021),

Proceedings of the Workshop on Multimodal Machine Learning in Low-resource Languages, pages 9 - 17
December 15, 2022 ©2022 Association for Computational Linguistics

five additional categories of neutral, ambiguous, anticipation, love, and trust are used in this study.

This research investigates Tamil YouTube comments to determine the emotions they represent. The primary purpose of this article is to investigate how effectively emojis assist in text emotion detection.

2 Prior Works

Prior works that used transformer-based models like Multilingual-BERT and XLM-R to to categorize Tamil YouTube comments into eleven emotions demonstrate how XML-R outperformed all other models with a macro F1-score of 0.33 (Mustakim et al., 2022). These multilingual transformers are also used to detect offensive hate and offensive content in Tamil YouTube comments (Rajalakshmi et al., 2023). The work details how the process of stemming and affix stripping makes a difference by giving better results in BERT inputs, especially in MuRIL. Prior works also focus on aspect-based and (Ganganwar and Rajalakshmi, 2019) and context aware sentiment with attention-enhanced features from bidirectional transformers (Sivakumar and Rajalakshmi, 2022). Various text embedding techniques/traditional algorithms are proposed, particularly for short text classification.(Rajalakshmi, 2014, 2015; Rajalakshmi and Aravindan, 2018; Rajalakshmi et al., 2018; Rajalakshmi and Xaviar, 2017; Rajalakshmi et al., 2020)

Multilingual BERT models like Indic Bert and XLMRoberta are used to detect offensive content in code-mixed Hindi-English tweets. Using them as embedding models with ensemble models as downstream classifiers seem to provide better performance than other classifiers (Rajalakshmi et al., 2021c). BERT based approaches see their usage not only in Tamil but also Arabic tweets. Including emoji in these approaches show an improvement in the performance of the models in identifying hate speech (Althobaiti, 2022). The work also states that the incorporation of textual emoji descriptions as features may enhance or degrade the performance of the models, depending on the number of examples per class and whether emojis are a distinguishing characteristic between classes. In previous works, sentiment analysis and span detection is performed using transformers models in code-mixed languages like Tamil-English and Hindi-English (Ravikiran et al., 2022)(Rajalakshmi et al., 2022c)(Rajalakshmi et al., 2021b)(Kannan et al., 2021).

Emoji embedding is one way to develop features for sentiment analysis tasks and can be seen in works that implement in Bi-LSTM based models for enhanced performace (Liu et al., 2021). Other works in Indian languages like Hindi and Marathi demonstrate the advantage of using XGBoost for multiclass classification (Rajalakshmi et al., 2021a). Sentiment analysis on the English Twitter dataset shows that the inclusion of emojis using TF-IDF as a feature extraction technique shows marginal improvement over excluding the emojis (Yoo and Rayz, 2021). Investigations show that a CNN can be used for emotion detection in Tamil when used with embedding approaches like BoW, TFIDF, Word2vec, fastText, and GloVe (Andrew, 2022). Moreover, there are works which focus on detecting signs of depression using XGBoost and detecting abusive comments in Tamil using transformer models from social media (Rajalakshmi et al., 2022a)(Sharen and Rajalakshmi, 2022).

The amount of emoji usage and the presence of text and emoji in expressing sentiments have been examined using the web documents of well-known male and female celebrities and compares the overall emoji usage among the most popular Twitter users (Gupta et al., 2020). The work demonstrates how sentiment analysis for both text and emoji is more thorough and accurate. Prior works also used other deep learning models like self-attentive LSTM, BiLSTM-CRF and hybrid convolutional bidirectional recurrent neural network for sentiment analysis (Sivakumar and Rajalakshmi, 2021)(Rajalakshmi et al., 2022b)(Soubraylu and Rajalakshmi, 2021).

3 Proposed Methodology

Understanding the function of emojis in Tamil text during sentiment analysis is the primary motivation behind this work. Tamil comments from YouTube are used as the input texts, which are preprocessed and vectorized using TF-IDF and MuRIL. Logistic Regression and

Notation	Emotion	Count	Notation	Emotion	Count
Joy	Joy	585	Ant	Anticipation	73
Neu	Neutral	401	Dis	Disgust	69
Tru	Trust	183	Ang	Anger	59
Lov	Love	143	Sur	Surprise	34
Amb	Ambiguous	139	Fea	Fear	12
Sad	Sadness	120			

Table 1: Dataset description

ensemble models like Random Forest and XGBoost are then trained on the features. Cross-validation is performed on the results and further analysis on the impact of emoji in text is discussed.

3.1 Dataset

The dataset consists of text from 22200 Tamil YouTube comments (Sampath et al., 2022). The text are classified into 11 different emotions: Neutral, Anger, Joy, Disgust, Trust, Anticipation, Ambiguous, Love, Surprise, Sadness and Fear. Some texts contain emojis while most of them don't. Since the primary focus of this research is to understand the role of emojis, the texts without emoji are removed and the dataset is constricted to 1818 texts with atleast one emoji. The description of the dataset and the notations used can be seen in Table 1. It can also be noticed that some texts in the dataset have one emoji, some have multiple emojis while others have the same emoji repeated multiple times.

3.2 Preprocessing

In an attempt to understand the contributions of emoji in a text, two additional input variations are considered for comparison. The first variation has no emoji and the other variation has the emojis name rather than the emoji itself. Figure 1 shows the example of the the input text variations. Another important thing to note down is that, emoji names for emojis with various skin tones are also mentioned down in the text with emoji name column. Further preprocessing is performed on all the columns with text. Stopword removal is done by utilizing the 125 stopwords suggested by Ashok R. (Ashok, 2016). An affix stripping iterative stemming algorithm (Porter, 2001) is used to reduce derivative words to their root form. After this, feature extraction of text takes place.

3.3 Feature Extraction

To vectorize the text data, this research employs two types of feature extraction techniques, TF-IDF and MuRIL. Further, cross-validation is performed on this vectorized data with a K-fold of 5.

3.3.1 TF-IDF

Term FrequencyInverse Document Frequency (TF-IDF) is employed for vectorizing the dataset. TF-IDF determines how pertinent a word is to a corpus or series of words in a text. The frequency of a term in the corpus offsets the way that meaning changes as a word appears more frequently in the text.

3.3.2 MuRIL

MuRIL is a pre-trained BERT model from Google's Indian research division (Khanuja et al., 2021). It is a multilingual language paradigm that has only been trained on corpora containing English and 16 additional Indian languages, including Tamil. Masked language modeling and translation language modeling are the two stages of training. Here, the MuRIL model is used as an embedding layer.

3.4 Classifiers

In this research, Logistic Regression, Random Forest and XGBoost are utilized to train the vectorized data. Hyperparameter tuning was performed for all classifiers and the parameters are presented in Table 2.

3.4.1 Logistic Regression

It is a machine learning model used for classification. The linear regression model is the source of its development. A logistic function is fitted with the output of the linear regression model to forecast the target variable. In this paradigm, a decision boundary is used. This

ID	Emotion	Text with Emoji	Text with Emoji name	Text without Emoji
143	Love	அந்த மனசு தான் கடவுள் 🎁🕊🤗	அந்த மனசு தான் கடவுள் [wrapped_gift][dove][smiling_face_with_open_hands]	அந்த மனசு தான் கடவுள்
185	Joy	மிக்க மகிழ்ச்சி அக்கா💕❤❤🙏🏼🙏🏼👌👌👌👋	மிக்க மகிழ்ச்சி அக்கா[two_hearts][red_heart][red_heart][folded_hands_medium-light_skin_tone][folded_hands_medium-light_skin_tone][OK_hand][OK_hand][OK_hand][waving_hand]	மிக்க மகிழ்ச்சி அக்கா
257	Sadness	ஆழ்ந்த இரங்கல் 😥😥	ஆழ்ந்த இரங்கல் [sad_but_relieved_face][sad_but_relieved_face]	ஆழ்ந்த இரங்கல்

Figure 1: Examples of input text variations

Classifier	Hyperparameter used
Logistics Regression	'C': 1, 'dual': False, 'fit intercept': False,
	, 'penalty': 'l2', 'solver':'newton-cg'
Random Forest	'bootstrap': True, 'class weight': None,
	, 'criterion': 'entropy', 'max features': 'log2',
	'n estimators': 100, 'oob score': False, 'warm start': False
XGBoost	'booster': 'gbtree', 'grow policy': 'depthwise',
	, 'learning rate': 0.1, 'max depth': 6,
	'sampling method': 'uniform', 'tree method': 'hist'

Table 2: Hyperparameters used for classifiers

establishes a cutoff point separating one class of variables from another.

3.4.2 Random Forest

It is an ensemble method, which entails combining numerous little decision trees, or estimators, each of which produces its own predictions. The random forest model incorporates the estimators' predictions to deliver a more precise prediction. Additionally, massive datasets with a variety of dimensions and feature types can be handled by random forests.

3.4.3 XGBoost

The gradient boosting framework is used by the decision tree-based ensemble machine learning method known as XGBoost. The XGBoost classifier is reliable and produces effective results in a variety of distributed situations. It also offers a wrapper class that enables models to be used in the scikit-learn framework as classifiers or regressors.

4 Results and Discussion

In this research, the evaluation metrics taken into account are weighted precision, weighted recall and weighted F1-Score. Since the dataset is imbalanced, weighted metrics are taken into account. While recall measures how effectively the positives are recognized, precision measures how accurately the predictions are made. F1-score is a culmination of the values of precision and recall.

It can be inferred from the Table 3 that both TF-IDF and MuRIL feature extraction methods achieve greater results when used with the XGBoost ensemble model. The XGBoost algorithm builds upon the Random Forest algorithm by introducing gradient boosting. By attempting to minimize error before adding further decision trees, the XGBoost algorithm (Chen and Guestrin, 2016) outperforms the Random Forest algorithm and thus in turn the Logistic Regression algorithm. It is also made abundantly clear that the presence of emojis in the text increases the performance. However, the way in which the emojis are represented also seems to play a role in the performance of the model. It can be noted that text with emoji receives a slightly better F1-score than plain text in both feature extraction scenarios. This may be explained by the fact that the addition of the emojis increases the feature space of the input vector, thus providing more information for the classifiers to train on.

It can be inferred that in both TF-IDF and MuRIL, text with emoji name has the best results. This could account to the fact that, when emojis are converted to its name state, it has more repetitive terms. For instance, the key word "Heart" appears in the phrases "Red Heart❤️", "Growing Heart💗", "Sparkling Heart💖", "Purple Heart💜", "Blue Heart💙", and so forth. The meaning of a heart is the same regardless of how it is shown in an emoji. Every emoji has a distinct unicode. This attributes to the fact that during vectorization, all these emojis are taken as unique features even when they have something in common. This issue is avoided when the emoji is converted to textual format, where more emphasis is given to each word while increasing the models performance.

Pre-trained transformer models generally perform well in NLP tasks. Their ability to do NSP (next sentence prediction) is used to learn the context between words, which can be used in a variety of tasks. Surprisingly Googles MuRIL transformer model trained on multilingual data including Tamil, fails to perform better than its TF-IDF counterpart when used as an embedding layer. The model overemphasizes one particular emotion, leading to all the predictions being that particular emotion and losing generalizability across the other emotions. This might be due to the imbalanced nature of the dataset. This case can also be viewed in Vaishali Ganganwar et al work where they proved that MuRIL showed underperformance due to dataset imbalance for Tamil text (Ganganwar and Rajalakshmi, 2022).

Figure 4 details the six most occurring emojis in the corpus taken and their occurrence across all emotions. Taking a look at the distribution of the emojis one can state that these popularly used emojis though being extensively used in two or three emotions are quite ambiguous and are used in unexpected emotions. The 🤣 emoji sees its main usage in the Joy emotion, which is to be expected as it represents rolling on the floor in laughter. However it also sees use in categories such as Ambiguous and Disgust which can confidently said is not represented by the emoji. From this it can be said that even though emojis can denote the emotion of the author of the text, they cannot be solely relied on and have to be used in combination with the words in the text. This is especially true in the case of sarcasm, where the emoji might denote an emotion which is not interpreted when one reads the entire text.

Another interesting area to draw insights from is the number of times an emoji is repeated. One might assume that the repetition of a single emoji multiple times in a text would be a strong indicator to a particular emotion. However, from table 5 it is evident that it is not the case. It is evident that the frequency of use of 2- and 3-repeating emojis against a single emoji differs. However, the coefficient of variance reveals that their distribution across all emotions is almost the same. To test the validity of this hypothesis that the distribution is same for all occurrences, a two sample t-test was performed on each pair of occurrences. The results of this test in Table 6 show that the p-value is greater than 0.05 for all occurrences. Thus we fail to reject the null hypothesis which signifies that the mean is not affected by the number of times emojis are repeated. This can also be seen in Figure 2 as the curves for the different occurrences have similar patterns even if they differ in magnitude. Thus it is noted that, the frequency of occurrence of an emoji in the text is not indicative of the conveyed emotion.

5 Conclusion and Future works

This study investigates the influence of emojis on the detection of emotion portrayed through Tamil YouTube comments. Text embedding was performed using TF-IDF and the MuRIL pre-trained model, while downstream classifiers included Logistic Regression, Random Forest, and XGBoost. The combination of TF-IDF and XGBoost yielded the best results, with a weighted-average F1 score of 0.32. Replacing the emoji with a word that represents it outperformed expressing it using UTF encoding

Feature Extraction	Category	LR			RF			XGBoost		
		P	**R**	**F1**	**P**	**R**	**F1**	**P**	**R**	**F1**
TF-IDF	Plain Text	0.24	0.29	0.25	0.23	0.29	0.24	0.25	0.31	**0.25**
	Text + Emoji	0.25	0.30	0.26	0.24	0.30	0.25	0.26	0.32	**0.26**
	Text + Emoji name	0.30	0.36	0.31	0.31	0.37	0.31	0.31	0.36	**0.32**
MuRIL	Plain Text	0.10	0.32	0.16	0.26	0.30	0.21	0.23	0.30	**0.24**
	Text + Emoji	0.10	0.32	0.16	0.26	0.32	0.23	0.25	0.31	**0.25**
	Text + Emoji name	0.10	0.32	0.16	0.23	0.33	0.22	0.29	0.35	**0.28**

Table 3: Performance of different classifiers on TF-IDF and MuRIL. Here, P represents Weighted Precision, R represents Weighted Recall and Weighted F1-Score.

Emoji	Occ	Joy	Neu	Tru	Lov	Amb	Sad	Ant	Dis	Ang	Sur	Fea
🙏	420	176	73	73	52	7	18	14	3	0	2	2
😂	211	86	47	6	3	16	4	8	22	8	9	2
👍	176	74	42	33	7	5	2	6	1	3	2	1
❤	96	40	13	12	22	2	2	3	0	2	0	1
🤣	96	41	1	3	1	10	1	1	8	6	4	2
😭	88	6	14	3	4	3	49	2	3	1	3	0

Table 4: Occurrence of the 6 most frequently used emojis and their distribution across all predicted emotions

Emoji	Occ	Coeff	Joy	Neu	Tru	Lov	Amb	Sad	Ant	Dis	Ang	Sur	Fea
🙏🙏🙏	162	0.1360	94	12	24	24	2	3	3	0	0	0	0
🙏🙏	60	0.1205	31	7	8	5	0	6	1	1	0	1	0
🙏	223	0.1371	131	31	34	13	3	8	1	1	0	0	1
👍👍👍	45	0.1445	28	7	6	1	1	1	0	0	0	1	0
👍👍	27	0.1644	19	6	2	0	0	0	0	0	0	0	0
👍	109	0.1343	61	19	20	2	0	1	3	1	1	0	1
❤❤❤	30	0.1346	14	5	0	11	0	0	0	0	0	0	0
❤❤	14	0.1229	7	1	3	2	0	0	1	0	0	0	0
❤	52	0.1334	30	3	7	7	1	1	2	0	1	0	0

Table 5: Analysis on the occurrence of emoji repetition

Test Condition	t	p	df	Diff	95% C.I.
🙏 vs 🙏🙏	1.2359	0.2308	20	14.82	-10.19 to 39.83
🙏 vs 🙏🙏🙏	0.3854	0.7040	20	5.55	-24.47 to 35.56
🙏🙏 vs 🙏🙏🙏	1.0500	0.3062	20	9.2	-9.15 to 27.69
👍 vs 👍👍	1.2761	0.2165	20	7.45	-4.73 to 19.64
👍 vs 👍👍👍	0.9521	0.3524	20	5.82	-6.93 to 18.57
👍👍 vs 👍👍👍	0.5364	0.5976	20	-1.64	-8.00 to 4.73
❤ vs ❤❤	1.2696	0.2188	20	3.45	-2.22 to 9.13
❤ vs ❤❤❤	0.6541	0.5205	20	2.00	-4.38 to 8.38
❤❤ vs ❤❤❤	0.8716	0.3938	20	-1.45	-4.94 to 2.03

Table 6: Statistics associated with number of times emoji used for expressing emotion intensity.

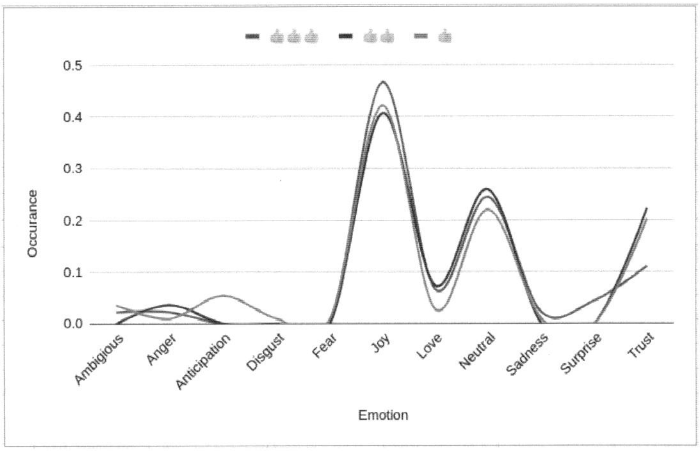

Figure 2: Repetition of 👍 in text and its normalized occurrence across all emotions.

or deleting it entirely from the text. The most often used emojis appear on text that convey an emotion very different to the one indicated by the emojis, demonstrating that one cannot rely just on these emojis to predict the emotion, but rather utilize them in conjunction with the text as has previously been shown useful. Repeated use of an emoji in the same text does not produce a greater link with any particular emotion than a single use of the same emoji as has been proved by a test of significance.

Because the introduction of social media and messaging applications has limited humans to utilizing text and emoticons as the primary mode of communication, this field of research has enormous promise. Emojis can give insight into the emotion that the author wishes to convey, but they can also be deceptive, thus other clues are necessary. More research may be done on the distinct combination of emojis and the emotion that they convey, as well as how they vary if the emojis were present independently. The dataset's imbalance was a big impediment, and working on a balanced dataset might provide better results. A bigger dataset with similar categories of emotions can be employed in future work to generalize findings from the study.

References

Francisca Adoma Acheampong, Chen Wenyu, and Henry Nunoo-Mensah. 2020. Text-based emotion detection: Advances, challenges, and opportunities. *Engineering Reports*, 2(7):e12189.

Maha Jarallah Althobaiti. 2022. Bert-based approach to arabic hate speech and offensive language detection in twitter: Exploiting emojis and sentiment analysis. *International Journal of Advanced Computer Science and Applications*, 13(5).

Judith Jeyafreeda Andrew. 2022. JudithJeyafreedaAndrew@TamilNLP-ACL2022:CNN for emotion analysis in Tamil. In *Proceedings of the Second Workshop on Speech and Language Technologies for Dravidian Languages*, pages 58–63, Dublin, Ireland. Association for Computational Linguistics.

R Ashok. 2016. Tamilnlp. `https://github.com/AshokR/TamilNLP/`.

Bharathi Raja Chakravarthi. 2020. HopeEDI: A multilingual hope speech detection dataset for equality, diversity, and inclusion. In *Proceedings of the Third Workshop on Computational Modeling of People's Opinions, Personality, and Emotion's in Social Media*, pages 41–53, Barcelona, Spain (Online). Association for Computational Linguistics.

Bharathi Raja Chakravarthi. 2022a. Hope speech detection in youtube comments. *Social Network Analysis and Mining*, 12(1):1–19.

Bharathi Raja Chakravarthi. 2022b. Multilingual hope speech detection in English and Dravidian languages. *International Journal of Data Science and Analytics*, 14(4):389–406.

Bharathi Raja Chakravarthi, Adeep Hande, Rahul Ponnusamy, Prasanna Kumar Kumaresan, and Ruba Priyadharshini. 2022. How can we detect homophobia and transphobia? experiments in a multilingual code-mixed setting for social media governance. *International Journal of Information Management Data Insights*, 2(2):100119.

Bharathi Raja Chakravarthi and Vigneshwaran Muralidaran. 2021. Findings of the shared task on hope speech detection for equality, diversity, and inclusion. In *Proceedings of the First Workshop on Language Technology for Equality, Diversity and Inclusion*, pages 61–72, Kyiv. Association for Computational Linguistics.

Tianqi Chen and Carlos Guestrin. 2016. Xgboost: A scalable tree boosting system. In *Proceedings of the 22nd acm sigkdd international conference on knowledge discovery and data mining*, pages 785–794.

Anthony Cherbonnier and Nicolas Michinov. 2021. The recognition of emotions beyond facial expressions: Comparing emoticons specifically designed to convey basic emotions with other modes of expression. *Computers in Human Behavior*, 118:106689.

Vaishali Ganganwar and R Rajalakshmi. 2019. Implicit aspect extraction for sentiment analysis: a survey of recent approaches. *Procedia Computer Science*, 165:485–491.

Vaishali Ganganwar and Ratnavel Rajalakshmi. 2022. MTDOT: A Multilingual Translation-based Data augmentation technique for Offensive content identification in Tamil text data. *Electronics*, 11(21).

Shelley Gupta, Archana Singh, and Jayanthi Ranjan. 2020. Sentiment analysis: usage of text and emoji for expressing sentiments. In *Advances in Data and Information Sciences*, pages 477–486. Springer.

Adeep Hande, Siddhanth U Hegde, and Bharathi Raja Chakravarthi. 2022. Multi-task learning in under-resourced dravidian languages. *Journal of Data, Information and Management*, 4(2):137–165.

R Ramesh Kannan, Ratnavel Rajalakshmi, and Lokesh Kumar. 2021. IndicBERT based approach for sentiment analysis on code-mixed Tamil tweets.

Simran Khanuja, Diksha Bansal, Sarvesh Mehtani, Savya Khosla, Atreyee Dey, Balaji Gopalan, Dilip Kumar Margam, Pooja Aggarwal, Rajiv Teja Nagipogu, Shachi Dave, et al. 2021. Muril: Multilingual representations for indian languages. *arXiv preprint arXiv:2103.10730*.

Chuchu Liu, Fan Fang, Xu Lin, Tie Cai, Xu Tan, Jianguo Liu, and Xin Lu. 2021. Improving sentiment analysis accuracy with emoji embedding. *Journal of Safety Science and Resilience*, 2(4):246–252.

Nasehatul Mustakim, Rabeya Rabu, Golam Md. Mursalin, Eftekhar Hossain, Omar Sharif, and Mohammed Moshiul Hoque. 2022. CUET-NLP@TamilNLP-ACL2022: Multi-class textual emotion detection from social media using transformer. In *Proceedings of the Second Workshop on Speech and Language Technologies for Dravidian Languages*, pages 199–206, Dublin, Ireland. Association for Computational Linguistics.

Martin F Porter. 2001. Snowball: A language for stemming algorithms.

R Rajalakshmi, Hans Tiwari, Jay Patel, Ankit Kumar, and R Karthik. 2020. Design of kids-specific URL classifier using Recurrent Convolutional Neural Network. *Procedia Computer Science*, 167:2124–2131.

R Rajalakshmi and Sanju Xaviar. 2017. Experimental study of feature weighting techniques for URL based webpage classification. *Procedia computer science*, 115:218–225.

Ratnavel Rajalakshmi. 2014. Supervised term weighting methods for URL classification. *J. Comput. Sci.*, 10(10):1969–1976.

Ratnavel Rajalakshmi. 2015. Identifying health domain URLs using SVM. In *Proceedings of the Third International Symposium on Women in Computing and Informatics*, pages 203–208.

Ratnavel Rajalakshmi and Chandrabose Aravindan. 2018. An effective and discriminative feature learning for URL based web page classification. In *2018 IEEE International Conference on Systems, Man, and Cybernetics (SMC)*, pages 1374–1379. IEEE.

Ratnavel Rajalakshmi, Ankita Duraphe, and Antonette Shibani. 2022a. DLRG@ DravidianLangTech-ACL2022: Abusive comment detection in tamil using multilingual transformer models. In *Proceedings of the Second Workshop on Speech and Language Technologies for Dravidian Languages*, pages 207–213.

Ratnavel Rajalakshmi, Faerie Mattins, S Srivarshan, and L Preethi Reddy. 2021a. Hate speech and offensive content identification in Hindi and Marathi language tweets using Ensemble techniques. pages 1 – 11. CEUR Workshop Proceedings.

Ratnavel Rajalakshmi, Mohit More, Bhamatipati Shrikriti, Gitansh Saharan, Hanchate Samyuktha, and Sayantan Nandy. 2022b. DLRG@ tamilnlp-acl2022: Offensive span identification in Tamil using BiLSTM-CRF approach. In *Proceedings of the Second Workshop on Speech and Language Technologies for Dravidian Languages*, pages 248–253.

Ratnavel Rajalakshmi, S Ramraj, and R Ramesh Kannan. 2018. Transfer learning approach for identification of malicious domain names. In *International Symposium on Security in Computing and Communication*, pages 656–666. Springer.

Ratnavel Rajalakshmi, Preethi Reddy, Shreya Khare, and Vaishali Ganganwar. 2022c. Sentimental analysis of code-mixed Hindi language. In *Congress on Intelligent Systems*, pages 739–751. Springer.

Ratnavel Rajalakshmi, Yashwant Reddy, and Lokesh Kumar. 2021b. DLRG@ dravidianlangtech-eacl2021: Transformer based approach for offensive language identification on code-mixed Tamil. In *Proceedings of the First Workshop on Speech and Language Technologies for Dravidian Languages*, pages 357–362.

Ratnavel Rajalakshmi, Srivarshan Selvaraj, Faerie Mattins R., Pavitra Vasudevan, and Anand Kumar M. 2023. HOTTEST: Hate and offensive content identification in Tamil using transformers and enhanced STemming. *Computer Speech Language*, 78:101464.

Ratnavel Rajalakshmi, S Srivarshan, Faerie Mattins, E Kaarthik, and Prithvi Seshadri. 2021c. Conversational Hate-offensive detection in code-mixed Hindi-English tweets. pages 1 –11. CEUR Workshop Proceedings.

Manikandan Ravikiran, Bharathi Raja Chakravarthi, Anand Kumar Madasamy, Sangeetha Sivanesan, Ratnavel Rajalakshmi, Sajeetha Thavareesan, Rahul Ponnusamy, and Shankar Mahadevan. 2022. Findings of the shared task on offensive span identification from code-mixed Tamil-English comments. *arXiv preprint arXiv:2205.06118*.

Anbukkarasi Sampath, Thenmozhi Durairaj, Bharathi Raja Chakravarthi, Ruba Priyadharshini, Subalalitha Cn, Kogilavani Shanmugavadivel, Sajeetha Thavareesan, Sathiyaraj Thangasamy, Parameswari Krishnamurthy, Adeep Hande, et al. 2022. Findings of the shared task on emotion analysis in Tamil. In *Proceedings of the Second Workshop on Speech and Language Technologies for Dravidian Languages*, pages 279–285.

Kogilavani Shanmugavadivel, Sai Haritha Sampath, Pramod Nandhakumar, Prasath Mahalingam, Malliga Subramanian, Prasanna Kumar Kumaresan, and Ruba Priyadharshini. 2022. An analysis of machine learning models for sentiment analysis of tamil code-mixed data. *Computer Speech & Language*, page 101407.

Herbert Sharen and Ratnavel Rajalakshmi. 2022. DLRG@ LT-EDI-ACL2022: Detecting signs of depression from social media using XGBoost method. In *Proceedings of the Second Workshop on Language Technology for Equality, Diversity and Inclusion*, pages 346–349.

Soubraylu Sivakumar and Ratnavel Rajalakshmi. 2021. Analysis of sentiment on movie reviews using word embedding self-attentive LSTM. *International Journal of Ambient Computing and Intelligence (IJACI)*, 12(2):33–52.

Soubraylu Sivakumar and Ratnavel Rajalakshmi. 2022. Context-aware sentiment analysis with attention-enhanced features from bidirectional transformers. *Social Network Analysis and Mining*, 12(1):1–23.

Sivakumar Soubraylu and Ratnavel Rajalakshmi. 2021. Hybrid convolutional bidirectional recurrent neural network based sentiment analysis on movie reviews. *Computational Intelligence*, 37(2):735–757.

Malliga Subramanian, Rahul Ponnusamy, Sean Benhur, Kogilavani Shanmugavadivel, Adhithiya Ganesan, Deepti Ravi, Gowtham Krishnan Shanmugasundaram, Ruba Priyadharshini, and Bharathi Raja Chakravarthi. 2022. Offensive language detection in tamil youtube comments by adapters and cross-domain knowledge transfer. *Computer Speech & Language*, 76:101404.

Sajeetha Thavareesan and Sinnathamby Mahesan. 2019. Sentiment analysis in tamil texts: A study on machine learning techniques and feature representation. In *2019 14th Conference on Industrial and Information Systems (ICIIS)*, pages 320–325. IEEE.

Sajeetha Thavareesan and Sinnathamby Mahesan. 2020a. Sentiment lexicon expansion using word2vec and fasttext for sentiment prediction in tamil texts. In *2020 Moratuwa Engineering Research Conference (MERCon)*, pages 272–276. IEEE.

Sajeetha Thavareesan and Sinnathamby Mahesan. 2020b. Word embedding-based part of speech tagging in tamil texts. In *2020 IEEE 15th International Conference on Industrial and Information Systems (ICIIS)*, pages 478–482. IEEE.

Byungkyu Yoo and Julia Taylor Rayz. 2021. Understanding emojis for sentiment analysis. In *The International FLAIRS Conference Proceedings*, volume 34.

Author Index